Walking With God

Biblical Foundations for New Believers

Russell Vance McFall

Copyright © 2026 by Russell McFall
All rights reserved.

No part of this publication may be reproduced, stored in a retrieval system, or transmitted in any form or by any means—electronic, mechanical, photocopying, recording, or otherwise—without prior written permission from the publisher, except for brief quotations used in reviews, articles, or scholarly works.

This book is a personal reflection on Scripture and spiritual truth. While every effort has been made to present Scripture accurately and respectfully, it is not intended as a formal or exhaustive commentary.

Published by **Ordained Path Books**
For permissions or inquiries, contact: **ordainedpathbooks@gmail.com**

Cover illustration and interior artwork generated by AI under the direction of the author.

First Edition

Scripture Note
Scripture quotations are taken from the New American Standard Bible® (NASB),
Copyright © 1960, 1971, 1977, 1995, 2020 by The Lockman Foundation. Used by permission. All rights reserved.

"Your word is a lamp to my feet
And a light to my path."
—Psalm 119:105 (NASB)

Ordained Path Books is dedicated to stories and resources that reflect timeless truth, courage, and the quiet strength of faith—guided by purpose and written to inspire.

ISBN (Paperback): 978-1-972724-16-3

Printed in the United States of America.

Version 1.02 — April 2026

Dedication

To those who are beginning their walk with God—
may you grow in clarity, confidence, and faith
as you learn to trust Him day by day.

Introduction

A Simple Beginning to Walking with God

If you are holding this book, there is a good chance you desire something more in your relationship with God.

Perhaps you have recently trusted in Christ and are wondering:

- "What comes next?"
- "How do I grow?"
- "How do I know I'm truly His?"

Or perhaps you have known the Lord for some time, yet still feel unsure in certain areas:

- Your assurance feels unsteady
- Your understanding feels incomplete
- Your growth feels inconsistent

You are not alone.

Many believers—new and seasoned alike—have walked through these same questions.

And the good news is this:

God has not left you to figure this out on your own.

A Relationship, Not a System

The Christian life is not meant to be complicated.

At its heart, it is a relationship.

It is not a system to master…

Not a list to complete…

Not a standard to perform your way into…

It is learning to walk with God.

That walk begins when you place your faith in Jesus Christ.

But it does not end there.

In many ways, that is where it truly begins.

Why This Book Exists

This book was written with a simple purpose:

To help you understand what God has said—and to help you walk with Him in a clear and steady way.

There are many helpful resources available today. Some are very detailed. Others are very practical.

Yet many believers still find themselves quietly asking:

- "Can someone just explain this simply?"
- "What does the Bible actually say about living the Christian life?"

This book is meant to help answer those questions.

Not with complicated language…

But with clear truth from Scripture.

What You Will Find Here

Each chapter focuses on a foundational truth of the Christian life.

These are not advanced topics.

They are the kind of truths that:

- strengthen your understanding
- steady your heart
- guide your daily walk

In each chapter, you will find:

- What Scripture says
- What it means in plain language

- How it applies to everyday life

You will also see examples—both from the Bible and from real experience—to help you recognize what these truths look like when lived out.

A Word About Growth

It is important to understand this from the beginning:

The Christian life is a process.

You will grow.

But growth does not happen all at once.

There will be:

- times of clarity
- times of struggle
- moments of confidence
- moments of doubt

None of this means something is wrong.

It means you are learning.

Just as a child learns to walk step by step, so you will learn to walk with God.

Take Your Time

This book is not meant to be rushed.

You may benefit most by:

- reading one chapter at a time
- reflecting on the Scripture
- thinking through the application

Some sections may speak to you more deeply than others.

That is normal.

You may even find yourself returning to certain chapters more than once.

That is part of the process.

A Final Encouragement

As you read, remember this:

You are not trying to earn your place with God.

If you have trusted in Christ, you already belong to Him.

This book is not about helping you become someone God will accept.

It is about helping you understand what He has already done—and how to walk in it.

Let's Begin

Wherever you are in your journey—whether just beginning or continuing forward—

You are invited to take the next step.

Not in your own strength…

But in dependence on the One who walks with you.

Contents

Dedication.....v
Introduction.....vi
Concept 1 — God's Love and His Plan.....1
Concept 2 — The Problem of Sin.....10
Concept 3 — God's Provision: Salvation Through Christ..18
*** Pause & Reflect ***.....27
Concept 4 — Assurance of Salvation.....30
Concept 5 — Identity in Christ.....40
Concept 6 — The Spiritual Life.....49
Concept 7 — The Word of God.....59
Concept 8 — Prayer.....69
Concept 9 — Fellowship.....78
Concept 10 — Witnessing.....86
Concept 11 — Obedience and Walking by Faith.....94
Concept 12 — Walking by the Spirit.....103
Conclusion - Continuing the Walk.....109
Appendix A — Key Bible Verses to Remember.....116
Appendix B — When You Struggle.....122
Appendix C — A Simple Guide to Prayer.....128
Appendix D — How to Begin Reading the Bible.....134
Where to Go From Here.....140
Continue Your Journey in the Bible.....144
How to Trust Jesus as Your Savior.....148
About the Author.....153
Also by Russell McFall.....154

Concept 1 — God's Love and His Plan

Understanding God's Heart Toward You

---

1. The Core Truth

God created you and loves you, and His desire is that you know Him personally—not just know about Him, but walk with Him in a real and lasting relationship.

---

2. What Scripture Says

• "*For God so loved the world, that He gave His only Son, so that everyone who believes in Him will not perish, but have eternal life.*" — John 3:16

• "*This is eternal life, that they may know You, the only true God, and Jesus Christ whom You have sent.*"
— John 17:3

• "*But God demonstrates His own love toward us, in that while we were still sinners, Christ died for us.*" — Romans 5:8

• "*I have loved you with an everlasting love; therefore I have drawn you with kindness.*" — Jeremiah 31:3

---

3. Understanding the Truth

When most people think about God, they often think in distant terms.

- A Creator
- A Judge
- Someone far removed

While it is true that God is holy and just, Scripture also reveals something deeply personal:

God loves.

Not in a general or distant way—

But in a personal and purposeful way.

Jesus said:

"For God so loved the world…"

That includes you.

Not because you earned it.

Not because you deserved it.

But because love is part of who He is.

This is important to understand:

God's desire is not simply that you follow rules.

His desire is that you know Him.

Jesus defined eternal life this way:

"That they may know You…"

Not just know about Him.

Not just believe certain truths.

But to know Him personally.

That changes how we see everything.

The Christian life is not first about:

- what you do

• how well you perform
• how much you accomplish

It is about a relationship that God Himself has made possible.

And like any relationship, it begins with trust.

From the very beginning, knowing God has always involved responding to Him by faith—trusting what He has said, even before everything is fully understood.

---

4. Why This Can Be Hard to Believe

Even though Scripture clearly teaches God's love, many people struggle to truly believe it.

A. We Often Measure Love by Human Experience

Our understanding of love is often shaped by:

• people
• relationships
• past experiences

And those experiences may include:

• disappointment
• inconsistency
• rejection

So when we hear that God loves us, we may quietly wonder:

"Is that really true for me?"

B. We Feel Unworthy

At times, we are very aware of our own shortcomings.

We may think:

• "God may love others…"
• "But He knows everything about me"
And because of that, we hesitate to believe that His love is real and personal.

C. We Think Love Must Be Earned
Many people assume:
"If God loves me, I must need to earn that love."
But Scripture shows the opposite.
"While we were still sinners, Christ died for us."
God's love is not a response to our goodness.
It is the reason He reaches out to us in the first place.

---

5. A Biblical Example

From the very beginning, we see God's desire for relationship.

In the account of Adam and Eve, God created man and woman not as distant beings, but to walk with Him.

There was fellowship.

There was closeness.

There was no separation.

But it is important to understand something clearly: the relationship that once existed without barrier is no longer what we naturally experience today.

There is now a separation.

Not always felt the same way by every person—
but real, nonetheless.

The Bible does not describe this as a small distance, but as something serious.

It affects how we know God,

how we respond to Him,

and ultimately where we stand before Him.

This separation is not only the result of what we do—

it reaches deeper than that.

The Bible shows that the problem is not merely that we have sinned, but that we are, by nature, separated from God.

Our thoughts, our desires, and our choices all reflect this condition.

At times we may try to improve ourselves,

or do what seems right—

but even then, something within us remains unchanged.

Left to ourselves, we cannot remove this separation.

And that is why this matters so deeply.

Left unresolved, this separation is not temporary.

It carries consequences beyond this life.

And yet—

even in the presence of that separation,

God's desire for relationship has not changed.

Jesus illustrated this beautifully in the story of the Prodigal Son.

A son turned away, chose his own path, and found himself far from home.

Yet when he returned, something unexpected happened.

The father did not reject him.

He did not keep his distance.

He ran to him.

He welcomed him.

He restored him.

This picture shows us something important:

God's heart is not to push people away—but to bring them near.

---

6. What This Looks Like in Daily Life

You may not always feel aware of God's love.

There may be times when:

- life feels difficult
- your thoughts are unsettled
- your heart feels distant

But God's love is not based on your awareness of it.

It is based on His nature.

There may also be times when you think:

- "I need to do better before I come to God"
- "I need to fix things first"

But the truth is:

You come to God because He loves you—not after you have made yourself acceptable.

In simple terms:

- You do not clean yourself up to come to God
- You come to God—and He begins the work in you
- Even this first step is taken by faith—simply trusting that His invitation is real and meant for you

---

7. God's Love Is the Beginning

It is important to understand this clearly:

God's love is not the result of your relationship with Him.

It is the reason for it.

He loved you first.

He reached out first.

He made the way for you to know Him.

Let this settle:

- You are not pursuing a reluctant God
- You are responding to a loving One

---

8. Common Misunderstandings

X "God's love must be earned"

No—God's love is given, not achieved.

X "God only loves people who live a certain way"

God's love is extended even while we are still sinners.

X "God is distant and uninterested"

God actively draws people to Himself.

X "I am the exception"

God's love is not limited—and you are not outside of it.

---

9. God's Provision / Key Insight

God has not only said that He loves you—

He has shown it.

He gave His Son.

He made a way for you to know Him.

He continues to draw you.

This means:

You are not trying to reach a distant God—

you are responding to One who has already come near.

---

10. A Simple Step to Begin

Take a few moments today and do something simple:

1. Read John 3:16 slowly
2. Replace "the world" with your own name
3. Consider what it means personally

Then thank God:

"Lord, thank You that Your love is real, and that You have made a way for me to know You."

But if God's desire is for relationship, it raises an important question:

Why does that relationship not always feel close or clear?

Why is there often a sense of distance—

even when we desire something more?

Scripture helps us understand that as well.

11. Linger Thought

You are not unknown to God—
and you are not unloved.
He has already set His love on you—
and He is inviting you to know Him.

Concept 2 — The Problem of Sin

Why We Are Separated from God

---

1. The Core Truth

Sin separates us from God, and it is not something we can overcome on our own. It affects who we are, how we live, and our relationship with Him.

---

2. What Scripture Says

• "*For all have sinned and fall short of the glory of God.*" — Romans 3:23

• "*For the wages of sin is death…*" — Romans 6:23

• "*But your wrongdoings have caused a separation between you and your God…*" — Isaiah 59:2

• "*And you were dead in your offenses and sins…*" — Ephesians 2:1–3

---

3. Understanding the Truth

If we are going to understand how to walk with God, we must first understand what has separated us from Him.

The Bible describes that problem with a single word:

Sin

Sin is often misunderstood.

Some think of it only as:

• major wrongdoing

• obvious moral failure

But Scripture shows that sin goes deeper than actions.

It is not just what we do.

It is part of our condition.

Sin includes:

• thoughts that are not aligned with God

• attitudes that resist Him

• actions that go against His ways

And because God is holy, sin cannot simply be ignored.

It creates a real separation.

Scripture says:

"All have sinned…"

That means:

• no one is exempt

• no one stands outside of this

It is not a problem for "some people."

It is a problem for all of us.

It may be helpful to consider this personally.

Have you ever told something that was not true—
even in a small way?

Have you ever taken something that did not belong to you—
even if it seemed insignificant?

Have there been thoughts, attitudes, or choices
that you knew were not right?

These questions are not meant to accuse—

but to help us see clearly.

By even our own understanding,

we recognize that something within us is not as it should be.

If we are honest, we do not need to look far to see this—

we can see it in our own lives.

And Scripture tells us that God's standard is not partial—

it is complete.

This is why the Bible says,

"All have sinned…"

Not in a distant or general sense—

but personally.

And because of that, it is not something we can overcome by effort or intention alone.

If there is to be a solution, it will not come from within us—but from God.

---

4. What Sin Does

It is helpful to understand not just what sin is—but what it does.

A. Sin Separates Us from God

God is holy.
That means He is completely pure and without sin.
Because of that, sin creates a barrier.
Scripture says:
"Your wrongdoings have caused a separation…"
This separation is not always something we feel—
but it is real.

B. Sin Affects Our Whole Life

Sin does not stay in one area.
It affects:

- how we think
- how we respond
- how we relate to others

It shapes our decisions—even in ways we may not recognize.

C. Sin Leaves Us Unable to Fix the Problem

Many people try to solve the problem of sin by:

- doing better
- trying harder
- improving their behavior

But Scripture says:
"You were dead in your offenses…"
This is a strong statement.
It means we are not simply struggling—
We are unable to fix ourselves.

---

5. A Biblical Example

We see the beginning of this problem in Adam and Eve.

They were created to walk with God.

There was no separation.

But when they chose to go their own way, something changed.

- Fellowship was broken
- Distance entered
- Fear replaced openness

They even hid from God.

That is what sin does.

We also see a powerful moment in the life of Isaiah.

When Isaiah saw the holiness of God, his response was immediate:

"Woe is me… for I am a man of unclean lips…"

In that moment, he became deeply aware of his own condition.

Not just his actions—

But his need.

---

6. What This Looks Like in Daily Life

You may recognize this in quiet ways.

There can be a sense of:

- distance from God
- unrest within
- a feeling that something is not right

You may try to address it by:

- improving your habits
- being more disciplined
- trying to do what is right

Those things may help in some ways.

But they do not remove the root problem.

At times, you may think:

- "If I can just do better, I will be okay"
- "If I try harder, things will change"

But sin is not just about effort.

It is about a condition that needs to be addressed at its core.

---

7. Let This Be Clear

This is important to understand—and to say carefully.

Sin is serious.

It separates us from God.

It affects every part of life.

And it is not something we can solve on our own.

But this is not where the story ends.

God does not reveal the problem to leave us there.

He reveals it so we will understand our need—and be ready to receive what He has done.

Understanding the problem is necessary—

Because it prepares us to understand the solution.

---

8. Common Misunderstandings

X **"I'm basically a good person"**

We may do good things, but Scripture says all have sinned.

X "Sin is only major wrongdoing"

Sin includes thoughts, attitudes, and actions.

X "I can fix this if I try hard enough"

Sin is not solved by effort alone.

X "This doesn't really apply to me"

Scripture makes it clear—this is a universal condition.

---

9. God's Provision / Key Insight

Even in describing sin, Scripture points us toward hope.

Why?

Because God does not reveal the problem to leave us there.

He reveals it so we will understand our need for Him.

And that we would be ready to trust what He provides—rather than trying to solve the problem ourselves.

You are not meant to carry this on your own.

You are meant to see clearly:

- the reality of sin
- the need for a solution
- and the inability to fix it yourself

---

10. A Simple Step to Begin

Take a few moments and reflect honestly:

- Where do you see this in your own life?
- Where do you sense distance or struggle?

Then respond with a simple prayer:

"Lord, help me to see clearly what You say about my need. Help me to understand this honestly and without turning away."

---

11. Linger Thought

The problem is deeper than behavior—
it is something within.
And until it is addressed,
nothing else will fully make sense.

Concept 3 — God's Provision: Salvation Through Christ

What God Has Done for You

---

1. The Core Truth

God has provided the solution to our sin through Jesus Christ. Salvation is not something we achieve—it is something we receive by faith in what He has already done.

---

2. What Scripture Says

- *"But God demonstrates His own love toward us, in that while we were still sinners, Christ died for us."* — Romans 5:8
- *"For by grace you have been saved through faith; and this is not of yourselves, it is the gift of God; not a result of works…"* — Ephesians 2:8–9
- *"For Christ also suffered for sins once for all, the righteous for the unrighteous, so that He might bring us to God…"* — 1 Peter 3:18
- *"Jesus said to him, 'I am the way, and the truth, and the life; no one comes to the Father except through Me.'"*
  — John 14:6

---

3. Understanding the Truth

In the previous chapter, we saw the reality of sin.

- It separates us from God
- It affects every part of life
- It is not something we can fix on our own

That leaves an important question:

"If I cannot fix this… then what can be done?"

Scripture answers that question clearly.

The answer is found in what God has done.

God did not leave us in our condition.

He did not wait for us to improve ourselves.

He acted —decisively and personally.

Scripture says:

"But God demonstrates His own love toward us…"

Not after we had changed—

Not after we had tried harder—

While we were still sinners

Christ died for us.

This was not a small act.

It was the cost of our sin placed upon Him.

This is the heart of the gospel.

Jesus Christ:

- lived a sinless life
- took upon Himself the penalty for sin
- died in our place
- rose again

He did for us what we could never do for

ourselves.

---

4. What This Means

It is important to understand this clearly:

Salvation is not based on:

- what you do
- how much you improve
- how consistent you are

It is based on:

- what Christ has already done

Scripture says:

"For by grace you have been saved through faith..."

Grace means:

- undeserved
- unearned

Faith means:

- trusting
- relying on

So salvation is:

Receiving what God has provided—by trusting in Christ, not in ourselves.

It is not:

- trying harder
- becoming better first
- proving yourself worthy

It is simply:

Trusting Him—

not in part, but completely.

---

5. Why This Can Be Hard to Accept

Even though this is simple, many people struggle to fully accept it.

A. We Want to Contribute Something

It feels natural to think:

- "I should do my part"
- "I need to earn this somehow"

But Scripture says:

"Not a result of works…"

There is nothing we can add to what Christ has done.

B. It Feels Too Simple

Some may think:

"It can't really be that simple."

But God's way is not complicated.

It is clear.

The difficulty is not in the message—

It is in our willingness to trust it.

C. We Focus on Ourselves Instead of Christ

We may ask:

- "Am I good enough?"
- "Have I done enough?"

But those are the wrong questions.

The focus is not on you.

It is on Christ.

---

6. A Biblical Example

We see a powerful example in the thief on the cross.

He had no opportunity to:

- correct his past
- perform good works
- demonstrate long-term change

Yet in a moment of simple faith, he turned to Jesus and said:

"Remember me…"

And Jesus responded:

"Today you will be with Me in Paradise."

That moment shows us something very important:

- Salvation is not based on a lifetime of effort
- It is based on faith in Christ

We also see this clearly in the question asked by the Philippian jailer in Acts 16:

"What must I do to be saved?"

The answer was simple:

"Believe in the Lord Jesus, and you will be saved."

---

7. What This Looks Like in Daily Life

You may find yourself thinking:

- "I need to get my life together first"
- "I need to be more consistent before I come to God"

But that is not what Scripture teaches.

You do not come to God after you fix yourself.

You come to God so that He can begin that work in you.

You may also wonder:

- "What does it mean to believe?"

It means:

- trusting Him
- relying on Him
- placing your confidence in Him

Not just agreeing with facts—

But trusting Him personally.

Trusting Him personally is the moment we are saved—brought into God's family once and for all.

From there, the life of faith continues—not to maintain salvation, but to grow in trust as we learn to follow Him more closely over time.

---

8. Let This Be Clear

Salvation is not:

- something you earn
- something you maintain
- something you deserve

It is:

A gift God freely gives through Jesus Christ.

And like any gift:

- It must be received

---

9. Common Misunderstandings

X "I need to clean myself up first"

You come to God as you are.

X **"I must earn my salvation"**

Salvation is by grace—not works.

X "Faith is just believing facts"

Faith is trusting Christ personally.

X "There are many ways to God"

Jesus said He is the way.

---

10. God's Provision / Key Insight

God has done everything necessary to bring you to Himself.

Nothing is missing.

Nothing needs to be added.

The question is not:

"What more must be done?"

The question is:

"Will I trust what He has done?"

Because that trust—simple and sincere—is what begins your walk with God.

11. A Simple Step to Begin

Understanding this leads to a personal decision.

If you have not yet done so, you can respond even now.

Becoming a Christian is not a long process—it is a moment of trust. In a simple and sincere way, you might say:

"Lord, I know that I cannot fix my sin on my own. I believe that Jesus died for me and rose again. I am trusting in Him alone as my Savior."

There are no special words required. It is not the words themselves that save you, but the trust of your heart—relying on Jesus Christ alone.

In that moment of faith, you are forgiven, given eternal life, and brought into God's family—once and for all.

12. Linger Thought

You are not saved by what you do for God—

but by what He has already done for you through Christ.

The Gospel:
A Simple Overview
GOD'S DESIGN
Created for Relationship with God
THE PROBLEM
GOD
SIN
MAN
Sin Separates Us from God
THE RESULT
We Cannot Fix This Ourselves
GOD'S PROVISION
Christ Paid for Our Sins
JESUS CHRIST
Christ Paid for Our Sins
THE RESPONSE
THE RESULT
Restored Relationship with God
By Grace Through Faith

*** Pause & Reflect ***

A Moment to Consider What You've Read

You have just read three important truths:

- God created you and loves you
- Sin has brought a real separation
- God has provided the solution through Jesus Christ

These are not just ideas to understand—
they are truths meant to be considered personally.
Take a few quiet moments and reflect.

---

1. What Have You Seen About God?

- Do you see that God's desire is for a relationship with you?
- Do you understand that His love is not based on your performance?

Take a moment to let this settle:
God has not moved away from you—
He has reached out to you.

---

2. What Have You Seen About Yourself?

• Do you recognize the reality of sin in your own life?

• Do you see that this is not only about actions—but about your condition?

• Do you understand that this separation cannot be removed by your own effort?

This is not meant to discourage you—
but to help you see clearly.

---

3. What Have You Seen About Christ?

• Do you understand that Jesus did for you what you could not do for yourself?

• Do you see that His death and resurrection provide the only way to be restored to God?

This is the heart of the message:
God has made a way.

---

4. What Are You Trusting In?

This is an important question.

• Are you trusting in your efforts?

• Your intentions?

• Your ability to improve?

Or—

• Are you trusting in what Jesus Christ has already done?

Salvation is not found in trying harder.
It is found in trusting Him.

---

5. Have You Responded?

Understanding these truths leads to a personal decision.

You do not need perfect words.

You do not need to prepare yourself first.

You simply respond by trusting Christ.

If that is the desire of your heart,

you may express it to God in your own words.

You might say something like:

"Lord, I see my need. I know that I cannot fix this on my own.

I believe that Jesus died for me and rose again.

I am trusting in Him alone as my Savior."

It is not the words that matter—

it is the trust of your heart.

---

6. A Quiet Encouragement

If you have placed your trust in Christ,

something real has taken place.

You are forgiven.

You are brought into a relationship with God.

You are no longer separated.

And this is just the beginning.

Linger Thought

God has not only shown you the truth—

He is inviting you to respond to it.

Take a moment.

Be honest.

And respond to Him.

Concept 4 — Assurance of Salvation

Knowing You Are His

---

1. The Core Truth

You can know with certainty that you belong to God—not because of how you feel, but because of what He has promised in His Word.

---

2. What Scripture Says

- *"And the testimony is this, that God has given us eternal life, and this life is in His Son. He who has the Son has the life… These things I have written to you… so that you may know that you have eternal life."* — 1 John 5:11–13
- *"My sheep hear My voice, and I know them, and they follow Me; and I give eternal life to them, and they will never perish… no one will snatch them out of My hand."* — John 10:27–29
- *"Therefore there is now no condemnation for those who are in Christ Jesus."* — Romans 8:1
- *"For I am convinced that neither death, nor life… nor any other created thing, will be able to separate us from the love of God, which is in Christ Jesus our Lord."* — Romans 8:38–39

3. Understanding the Truth

One of the most common—and often quiet—struggles in the Christian life is this question:

"How can I know that I am truly saved?"

For many, this question does not come just once.

It returns at different times and in different ways.

It may come:

• After a failure you regret

• When your heart feels distant

• When your emotions seem flat

• When you compare yourself to someone who appears stronger

And in those moments, the question can feel very real:

"Did anything really happen?"

"Am I truly His?"

God does not intend for you to live in uncertainty.

He answers this question directly in His Word.

Notice what He says:

"These things I have written… so that you may know…"

He does not say:

• hope

• guess

• assume

He says:

know

That word is meant to settle your heart.

Your assurance is not meant to be uncertain or fragile.

It is meant to rest on something unchanging—God Himself.

When you trusted in Christ, something real took place.

Not something based on emotion.

Not something temporary.

Something eternal.

A simple illustration may help.

When a man and woman are married, they often express that commitment with the words, "I do."

Those words are not just a formality—they are the expression of a decision. An act of the will. In that moment, they enter into a real relationship.

Their feelings at that moment may vary. They may feel great joy, or they may feel nervous or overwhelmed. But the marriage itself is not based on how strongly they feel—it is based on the commitment that was made.

In a similar way, becoming a Christian is not based on a certain feeling. It is based on a real moment when a person places their trust in Jesus Christ.

Like saying "I do," faith is the response of the heart—relying on Him alone as Savior.

From that moment on, your assurance does not rest on changing emotions, but on the unchanging promise of God.

And just as it was received by faith, it is also understood and rested in by faith—trusting what God has said, even when feelings are unsettled.

---

4. Why We Sometimes Doubt

Even true believers can struggle with assurance.

Understanding why this happens can help you respond rightly when doubt comes.

A. Feelings Change

There are days when you feel close to God.

There are other days when:

- You feel distant
- Your heart feels quiet
- Your emotions are not strong

If your assurance is based on feelings, it will rise and fall constantly.

But God never intended your assurance to rest on your emotions.

B. Sin Affects Our Confidence

When we sin, it can bring:

- Guilt
- Shame
- A sense of distance

Instead of running to God, we may begin to pull back.

And the thought comes:

"Maybe I'm not really saved."

But Scripture says:

"There is now no condemnation for those who are in Christ Jesus."

Your failure does not undo what Christ has already done for you.

C. Looking Inward Instead of Upward

We often evaluate ourselves by asking:

- "Am I doing well enough?"
- "Do I feel different enough?"

But assurance is not found by measuring yourself.
It is found by trusting Christ.

D. Lack of Clear Understanding

Some believers have never been clearly shown from Scripture how to have assurance.
So they live in uncertainty—not because they are not saved—but because they have not yet been grounded in truth.

E. Confusing Growth with Perfection

Sometimes we assume:
"If I were truly saved, I would be further along by now."
We compare ourselves to others and think:

- "They seem stronger"
- "They seem more consistent"

And then quietly:
"Maybe something is wrong with me."
But growth in the Christian life is not instant.
It is gradual.
Like a child learning to walk, there are:

- steps
- stumbles
- progress over time

Your assurance is not based on how far you have

come—

It is based on the One who saved you.

---

5. A Biblical Example

The apostle Thomas gives us a very honest picture of doubt.

After the resurrection, Thomas said he would not believe unless he could see and touch the wounds of Christ.

This was not a small hesitation—it was a deep struggle.

Yet when Jesus appeared to him, He did not reject Thomas.

He met him.

He showed him the truth.

And Thomas responded in faith.

His story reminds us:

- Doubt can be real
- But it does not have to remain

Assurance grows as we turn our eyes from our uncertainty and look again to Christ.

We also see this in Abraham.

God made a promise to him—one that seemed impossible.

Yet Scripture tells us:

"He did not waver in unbelief… but grew strong in faith…"

Abraham's confidence was not in himself.

It was in the One who made the promise.

That is the same foundation for your assurance.

A Simple and Clear Example

In Acts 16, a man asked a direct question:

"What must I do to be saved?"

The answer was just as direct:

"Believe in the Lord Jesus, and you will be saved."

There was no uncertainty.

No long list of conditions.

Salvation—and assurance—rest on the same truth:

Trusting what God has said about His Son.

---

6. What This Looks Like in Daily Life

There will be days when your faith feels strong.

There will also be days when it does not.

You may find yourself thinking:

- "I haven't been consistent."
- "I failed again."
- "I don't feel close to God."

And then quietly:

"Maybe I'm not really His."

In that moment, everything can feel uncertain.

But that is exactly when truth matters most.

Instead of following those thoughts further, pause and ask:

- "What has God said?"
- "What does His Word declare?"

Then return to what is unchanging:

- Christ has paid for your sin
- God has given you eternal life
- His promise does not change

Your relationship with God is not fragile.

It is not based on how you performed this week.
It rests on the finished work of Jesus Christ.

---

7. God's Promise Is the Anchor

Let this settle clearly in your heart:

- Your salvation was not earned by your effort
- It is not maintained by your effort
- And it is not lost by your weakness

It was secured by Christ.
And what He has secured—
He does not undo.
Scripture says:
"He who has the Son has the life…"
The question is not:
"Have I done enough?"
The question is:
"Do I have the Son?"

That is a question answered by faith—trusting God's Word over your own uncertainty.

If you have trusted Christ:

- You have life
- You belong to Him
- You are secure in Him

Jesus said:
"No one will snatch them out of My hand."
Not others.
Not circumstances.
Not even your own weakness.
Your security is not in your grip on Him—
It is in His grip on you.

---

8. Common Misunderstandings

X "I don't feel saved, so I must not be"
Feelings change. God's truth does not.

X "If I were truly saved, I wouldn't struggle"
Every believer is growing. Struggle does not cancel salvation.

X "I need to prove myself to stay saved"
Salvation is not maintained by effort—it is secured by Christ.

X "Assurance comes from how well I'm doing"
Assurance comes from trusting what Christ has already done.

---

9. God's Provision / Key Insight

God has given you everything you need for assurance:

- His **Word** — so you can know
- His **promises** — so you can trust
- His **Son** — so you can be saved

Your confidence is not found in holding tightly to Him—

It is found in trusting that **He is holding you.**

---

10. A Simple Step to Begin

When doubt comes—and it will—respond intentionally:

1. Turn to 1 John 5:11–13
2. Read it slowly
3. Notice the words "you may know"
4. Thank God for His promise

You might pray:

"Lord, thank You that my salvation is based on Your Word, not my feelings. Help me to rest in what You have said."

---

11. Linger Thought

You do not need to live wondering where you stand with God—He has already made it clear through His Word.

Concept 5 — Identity in Christ

Understanding Who You Are Now

---

1. The Core Truth

When you place your faith in Christ, you are not only forgiven—you are made new. Your identity is no longer defined by your past, your failures, or your feelings, but by your relationship with Him.

---

2. What Scripture Says

- *"Therefore if anyone is in Christ, this person is a new creation; the old things passed away; behold, new things have come."* — 2 Corinthians 5:17
- *"I have been crucified with Christ; and it is no longer I who live, but Christ lives in me…"* — Galatians 2:20
- *"Blessed be the God and Father… who has blessed us with every spiritual blessing in the heavenly places in Christ…"* — Ephesians 1:3–7
- *"…in Him you have been made complete…"* — Colossians 2:9–10

---

3. Understanding the Truth

After you have come to understand that you belong to God, a new question naturally follows:

"Now that I am His… who am I?"

Assurance settles your standing with God.

Identity begins to shape how you live in that relationship.

If assurance answers:

"Am I truly His?"

Then identity answers:

"What has changed because I am His?"

These two truths are meant to be held together.

You are secure in Christ—

and now you are learning to live in who you are in Him.

Before coming to Christ, your identity may have been shaped by many things:

- Your past
- Your failures
- Your accomplishments
- What others said about you
- How you saw yourself

But when you trusted in Christ, something profound happened.

You were not simply improved.

You were **made new.**

Scripture does not say:

- "You are becoming a new creation someday"

It says:

"**You are a new creation**."

This may take time to fully understand.

That is part of your growth.

That is not a feeling.

It is not a goal.

It is a **fact established by God**.

And like many things in the Christian life, it is something you come to understand more fully by faith—trusting what God says, even before you fully see it in your experience.

This change is not something you must earn or maintain.

It is something God has already done.

Even if you do not fully understand it yet…

Even if you do not always feel it…

It is still true.

And learning to believe that truth is part of your growth.

Yet many believers continue to live as though nothing has changed.

They still define themselves by:

- past sin
- old labels
- personal weakness

And because of that, they struggle to grow.

Because we tend to live in a way that matches what we believe about ourselves.

And that is why it is so important to see yourself the way God sees you.

Not with pressure…

But with clarity.

---

4. Why We Struggle to See This Clearly

Even though this truth is clearly taught in Scripture, many believers struggle to fully embrace it.

A. The Past Feels More Real Than the Present

You may think:

- "I know what I've done"
- "I know who I used to be"

Those memories can feel more real than what God says.

But your identity is not determined by your past.

It is determined by what Christ has done.

B. Feelings Do Not Always Reflect Truth

There may be days when you do not feel different.

You may still struggle with:

- the same habits
- the same thoughts
- the same weaknesses

And you may think:

"Nothing has really changed."

But identity is not based on how you feel.

It is based on what God has declared.

C. Confusing Position with Practice

This is very important.

Your **position:**

- Who you are in Christ
- Complete, accepted, secure

Your **practice**:

- How you live day by day
- Still growing
- Still learning

These are not the same.

You may not yet live perfectly according to your identity—

But that does not change who you are.

---

5. A Biblical Example

The apostle Paul is one of the clearest examples of identity transformation.

Before coming to Christ:

- He persecuted believers
- He opposed the message of Jesus

After coming to Christ:

- He became a servant of the very message he once fought

But notice something important:

Paul did not continue to define himself by his past.

Instead, he wrote:

"It is no longer I who live, but Christ lives in me."

His identity was no longer rooted in who he had been—

But in who he now was in Christ.

We also see this in Zacchaeus.

He had been known as:

- dishonest
- greedy
- rejected

But after encountering Jesus, his life began to

change.

His actions started to reflect a new identity.

He was no longer defined by his past—

He was changed by his relationship with Christ.

A Simple Picture

Imagine someone who has been given a completely new name and a new place in a family.

Legally, it is done.

They belong.

But it may take time for them to:

- think differently
- act differently
- fully understand what that means

That is what happens in the Christian life.

You are already changed—

But you are learning to live in that change.

---

6. What This Looks Like in Daily Life

There may be moments when you find yourself thinking:

- "I'm just not the kind of person who can live this way"
- "I always struggle with this"
- "This is just who I am"

But those thoughts are often rooted in your old identity.

In those moments, gently pause and ask:

- "What has God said about me?"
- "What is true in Christ?"

Then remind yourself:

- "In Christ, I am new"
- "In Christ, I am forgiven"
- "In Christ, I am accepted"

This is not pretending —it is learning to agree with what God has already said.

It is aligning your thinking with truth.

It is choosing, by faith, to agree with what God has said about you.

Take a moment to let this settle:

You are not trying to become someone new.

In Christ—

You already are.

And your life now is a process of learning to walk in what God has already made true.

---

7. God's Declaration About You

Scripture makes clear statements about who you are in Christ:

- You are **forgiven**
- You are **accepted**
- You are **brought near to God**
- You are **complete in Christ**

These are not future promises only.

They are present realities.

You may still be growing.

But you are not unfinished in your standing before God.

You are fully accepted—right now.

---

8. Let This Settle Clearly

It is important to say this plainly:

- You are not trying to become someone God will accept
- You are learning to live as someone He already has accepted

Your identity is not something you achieve.

It is something you receive.

And you continue to receive it in the same way—by faith, learning to believe what God has already made true.

Because of that:

- You do not live for acceptance
- You live from acceptance

That changes everything.

---

9. Common Misunderstandings

X "I'm still who I used to be"

No—you have been made new in Christ.

X "I need to feel different to be different"

Truth does not depend on feelings.

X "My past defines me"

Your past is real—but it no longer defines you.

X "I have to earn my place with God"

Your place with God is already secured in Christ.

---

10. God's Provision / Key Insight

God has not only saved you—
He has given you a new identity.
And He is now at work in you to help you:

- understand it
- believe it
- live it out

This is not something you must create.
It is something you are learning to see clearly.

---

11. A Simple Step to Begin

Take a few moments today:

1. Read 2 Corinthians 5:17 slowly
2. Replace "anyone" with your name
3. Say it out loud

Then thank God:

"Lord, thank You that in Christ, I am a new creation. Help me to live in the truth of what You have already done."

---

12. Linger Thought

You belong to Him—
and you are learning to live in who you are in Christ

You belong to Him—
and you are being shaped by who you are in Christ.

Concept 6 — The Spiritual Life

Learning to Walk with God Day by Day

---

1. The Core Truth

The Christian life is not lived by your own strength, but by learning to depend on the Holy Spirit day by day—walking with God by faith.

---

2. What Scripture Says

- "*But I say, walk by the Spirit, and you will not carry out the desire of the flesh.*" — Galatians 5:16
- "*For all who are being led by the Spirit of God, these are sons of God.*" — Romans 8:14
- "*So then, my beloved… work out your salvation with fear and trembling; for it is God who is at work in you…*" — Philippians 2:12–13
- "*Are you so foolish? Having begun by the Spirit, are you now being perfected by the flesh?*" — Galatians 3:3

---

3. Understanding the Truth

After understanding that you are secure in Christ and that you have a new identity in Him, a very practical question naturally follows:

"How do I live this out every day?"

Many believers begin well.

They trust in Christ.

They understand the gospel.

But then, without realizing it, they begin to live the Christian life the same way they lived before—

by relying on themselves.

They think:

- "I need to try harder"
- "I need to be more disciplined"
- "I need to get this right"

And while effort and discipline have their place, the Christian life is not sustained by effort alone.

Scripture asks a very direct question:

"Having begun by the Spirit, are you now being perfected by the flesh?"

The answer is no.

The same way you began—

by depending on God—

is the same way you continue.

The Christian life is not about becoming independent and strong on your own.

It is about learning to live in **dependence.**

---

4. Three Ways People Live

The Bible helps us understand this by describing three kinds of people.

These are not labels to judge others—but truths to help us understand ourselves.

A. The Natural Person

This is someone who has not trusted Christ.

- Lives apart from God
- Relies on human understanding

"A natural person does not accept the things of the Spirit of God…" — 1 Corinthians 2:14

B. The Carnal Christian

This is a believer—but one who is living in self-dependence.

- Saved
- But not growing as they could
- Often controlled by old patterns

"I… could not speak to you as to spiritual men, but as to men of flesh…" — 1 Corinthians 3:1–3

C. The Spiritual Christian

This is a believer who is learning to depend on the Holy Spirit.

- Not perfect
- But growing
- Increasingly responsive to God

"The spiritual person evaluates all things…" — 1 Corinthians 2:15

It is important to understand:

These are not permanent categories.

A believer may move between these depending on whether they are relying on themselves or on God.

---

5. What It Means to Walk by the Spirit

To "walk by the Spirit" is not a complicated idea.

It simply means:

- depending on God
- trusting Him in your daily life
- responding to His leading through His Word

It is not a feeling.

It is not something distant or mysterious.

It is a steady, daily way of living.

---

6. Living by Faith — From Beginning to Daily Life

When you first came to Christ, you came by faith.

You did not earn your salvation.

You did not achieve it through effort.

You trusted in what Christ had done for you.

Scripture says:

"For by grace you have been saved through faith…"

That is how the Christian life begins.

But it is important to understand this:

The Christian life is not only begun by faith—
it is lived by faith.

Sometimes we begin to think:

- "I was saved by faith… now I must live by effort."

But that is not what Scripture teaches.

Just as you trusted Christ for your salvation—
You continue to trust Him in your daily life.

Scripture says:

"But my righteous one shall live by faith…" — Romans 1:17

This touches every part of life.

We Trust Him Day by Day

- When you are uncertain → you trust Him
- When you are weak → you trust Him
- When you do not understand → you trust Him

We Love Others by Faith

There are times when loving others does not come naturally.

In those moments, you may feel:

"I don't have the ability to do this."

And in your own strength, that may be true.

So you respond by faith:

"Lord, help me to love this person as You would."

And you move forward trusting Him to work through you.

We Obey by Faith

There are times when obedience is difficult.

- You may not feel ready
- You may not feel strong

But faith does not wait for perfect conditions.

It responds to what God has said.

We Grow by Faith

Even your growth is not something you produce on your own.

You trust that:

- God is at work in you
- He is shaping you over time

---

7. Why This Can Be Difficult

Even though this is simple, it is not always easy.

A. We Naturally Rely on Ourselves

From a young age, we learn to:

- solve problems
- take control
- depend on our own abilities

So it feels natural to try to live the Christian life the same way.

B. We Expect Immediate Growth

We may think:

- "I should be further along by now"
- "I shouldn't struggle like this"

But growth takes time.

C. We Become Discouraged by Failure

When we fail, we may think:

"I'm not doing this right."

And instead of returning to dependence on God, we try harder in our own strength.

---

8. A Biblical Example

We see this clearly in the life of Peter.

Peter sincerely desired to follow Jesus.

At one point, he said:

"Even if everyone else falls away, I will not."

He was confident—but that confidence was in himself.

And when pressure came, he failed.

He denied the Lord.

But that was not the end of his story.

Jesus restored him.

And over time, Peter learned something important:

The Christian life is not lived through self-confidence—

but through dependence on God.

We also see this in Paul.

Paul was greatly used by God, yet he wrote:

"My grace is sufficient for you, for power is perfected in weakness."

Paul learned that weakness was not something to eliminate—

It was the place where God's strength became clear.

---

9. What This Looks Like in Daily Life

This becomes very practical.

There may be moments when you feel:

- frustrated

- tempted
- uncertain
- overwhelmed

In those moments, you have a choice:

- rely on yourself
- or turn to God

Walking by the Spirit often looks like something simple:

- pausing
- acknowledging your need
- asking for God's help
- moving forward in trust

You may think:

- "I've tried this before and failed"

But the Christian life is not about never failing.

It is about:

returning again and again to dependence on God.

---

10. Let This Settle Clearly

You did not begin the Christian life by trusting yourself.

And you are not meant to continue it that way.

- You are not expected to carry this alone
- You were never meant to live this life by your own strength

Scripture says:

"It is God who is at work in you…"

That means:

- you are not alone
- you are not unsupported
- you are not responsible for producing change by yourself

You are learning to cooperate with what God is already doing.

---

11. Common Misunderstandings

X **"I just need to try harder"**

The Christian life is not sustained by effort alone.

X "If I struggle, something is wrong"

Struggle is part of growth.

X "Spiritual people don't fail"

Spiritual growth includes failure and restoration.

X "I should be able to do this on my own"

You were never meant to.

---

12. God's Provision / Key Insight

God has given you everything you need to live this life:

- His Spirit — to guide and empower
- His Word — to instruct and direct
- His grace — to restore when you fail

The Christian life is not about becoming strong on your own.

It is about learning to depend on Him more fully—by faith.

---

13. A Simple Step to Begin

Today, take one simple step:

When you face something difficult, pause and pray:

"Lord, I cannot do this on my own. I am trusting You to help me right now."

Then move forward—

Not in confidence in yourself,

but in faith in Him.

---

14. Linger Thought

You are not called to live the Christian life for God—

you are called to live it with Him.

And just as you came to Him by faith—

you now walk with Him the same way.

Concept 7 — The Word of God

Hearing God Speak and Learning to Trust What He Says

---

1. The Core Truth

God speaks to us through His Word, and as we learn to trust and respond to it by faith, it shapes our thinking, guides our decisions, and strengthens our walk with Him.

---

2. What Scripture Says

- *"All Scripture is inspired by God and beneficial for teaching, for rebuke, for correction, for training in righteousness…"* — 2 Timothy 3:16–17
- *"Your word is a lamp to my feet and a light to my path."* — Psalm 119:105
- *"For the word of God is living and active…"* — Hebrews 4:12
- *"Sanctify them in the truth; Your word is truth."* — John 17:17

---

3. Understanding the Truth

If the Christian life is a walk with God, then a natural question is:

"How does God guide me in that walk?"

The answer is not found in guessing, or in trying to figure everything out on your own.

The answer is found in what God has already spoken.

God speaks to us through His Word.

This is important to understand—and to take in slowly.

The Bible is not just:

- a collection of writings
- a historical record
- a book of helpful ideas

It is:

God's Word given to us

Scripture says:

"All Scripture is inspired by God…"

That means it is not simply human thought.

It is God revealing:

- who He is
- what is true
- how we are to live

So when you open the Bible, you are not just reading information.

You are being given truth from God.

You may not always feel that right away.

You may read and think:

- "I'm not sure I understand this fully"
- "I'm not sure what to take from this yet"

But even in those moments:

God's Word is still true

and it is still working in your life

---

4. Why This Matters

As you learn to walk with God, you will face many questions:

- "What should I do?"
- "What is right?"
- "How should I respond?"

God has not left you without direction.

He has given you His Word as a guide.

Scripture says:

"Your word is a lamp to my feet and a light to my path."

A lamp does not show everything at once.

It gives light for the next step.

And that is how God often leads.

Not by showing the entire future—

but by giving clarity for the next step as you trust Him

---

5. A Biblical Example

We see this clearly in the life of Jesus Christ.

When He was tempted, He did not rely on personal strength alone.

He responded with Scripture:

"It is written…"

Again and again, He turned to God's Word.

Not just as knowledge—

but as truth to stand on

We also see this in Ezra.

Scripture tells us that Ezra had set his heart to:

- study the Word
- practice it
- teach it

The Word of God shaped his thinking, his actions, and his direction.

These examples show us:

God's Word is not just something we read—

it is something we live by

---

6. Receiving God's Word by Faith

Just as you came to Christ by faith…
You now receive His Word the same way

There will be times when:

- you do not fully understand
- you do not feel the impact immediately
- you are unsure how it applies

And in those moments, it can be tempting to think:
"Maybe this isn't helping"

But the Word of God does not depend on your feelings to be true.

So you respond by faith:

- trusting that what God has said is true
- choosing to believe it
- allowing it to shape your thinking over time

Scripture says:
"Your word is truth."

Not sometimes.
Not only when it feels clear.
Always.

And over time, as you continue, something begins to change.

- your thinking becomes clearer

- your responses begin to shift
- your understanding grows

Often slowly.
But steadily.

---

7. Why This Can Be Difficult

Even though God's Word is available to us, it is not always easy to stay consistent.

A. Life Feels Busy

There are always things competing for your attention.
And time in God's Word can easily be set aside.

B. You May Not Feel Immediate Results

You may read and think:
"I'm not sure I'm getting much from this."

But growth is often gradual.
The Word is shaping you—
even when you do not see it right away

C. You May Feel Uncertain About Understanding

You may wonder:

- "Am I understanding this correctly?"
- "Where do I begin?"

That is normal.
Understanding grows over time.

---

8. What This Looks Like in Daily Life

This becomes very practical.

Spending time in God's Word is not about:

- checking a box
- reading large amounts
- trying to master everything at once

It is about:

consistently coming to God and listening

It may feel simple.

And sometimes it will feel small.

But over time, it becomes steady.

This might look like:

- reading a short passage
- thinking about what it says
- asking, "What does this show me about God?"
- considering how it applies

And then responding by faith:

- trusting what you have read
- taking a simple step to live it out

These small, consistent moments matter more than you may realize.

---

9. Let This Settle Clearly

You do not need to have complete understanding to begin.

You do not need to feel something every time.

You do not need to be perfect in consistency.

What matters is this:

You are coming to God,

and you are learning to trust what He has said

And over time:

- your thinking will change
- your perspective will grow
- your walk will become steadier

---

10. Common Misunderstandings

X "The Bible is too difficult, so I'll wait"

Understanding grows over time—you can begin now.

X "I need to feel something for it to matter"

Truth is still working, even when feelings are quiet.

X "Reading alone is enough"

The goal is not just reading—but trusting and responding.

X "I must understand everything immediately"

Growth in understanding is a process.

---

11. God's Provision / Key Insight

God has not left you without guidance.

He has given you His Word so that you can:

- know what is true
- understand His ways
- walk with clarity

And just as you came to Him by faith—

you continue to walk by trusting what He has said

---

12. A Simple Step to Begin

Start with something simple:

1. Choose a short passage
2. Read it slowly
3. Ask:
   - o What does this show me about God?
   - o What is one thing I can trust here?
4. Respond in a simple way

You might pray:

"Lord, help me to understand Your Word and to trust what You have said."

And as you learn to listen to God through His Word,

you will also find yourself wanting to respond to Him

13. Linger Thought

God has spoken—
and His Word is steady and true.
As you trust it,
it will guide your steps.

Concept 8 — Prayer

Talking with God by Faith

---

1. The Core Truth

Prayer is simply talking with God. It is not based on special words or performance, but on coming to Him in faith—trusting that He hears you and cares for you.

---

2. What Scripture Says

- *"Call to Me and I will answer you, and I will tell you great and mighty things…"* — Jeremiah 33:3
- *"Be anxious for nothing, but in everything by prayer and pleading with thanksgiving let your requests be made known to God."* — Philippians 4:6
- *"And this is the confidence which we have before Him, that, if we ask anything according to His will, He hears us."* — 1 John 5:14
- *"And when you pray, do not use meaningless repetition… for your Father knows what you need before you ask Him."* — Matthew 6:7–8

---

3. Understanding the Truth

If God speaks to us through His Word, then prayer is how we respond.

It is how we:

- speak with Him
- bring our thoughts to Him
- share what is on our hearts

Prayer is not meant to be complicated.

It is not:

- a performance
- a formula
- a set of perfect words

It is:

a conversation with God

And like any conversation, it grows over time.

It does not need to be perfect to be real.

This is important to understand.

Because many people feel uncertain about prayer.

They may think:

- "I don't know what to say"
- "I'm not sure I'm doing it right"
- "My prayers don't sound like others"

And sometimes, even after praying, you may feel:

- "Did that matter?"
- "Was that enough?"

But God is not looking for polished words.

He is inviting you to come to Him.

---

4. Coming to God by Faith

Just as you came to Christ by faith…

You come to God in prayer the same way.

You do not see Him with your eyes.

You do not hear His voice audibly.

Yet you trust:

- that He is there
- that He hears
- that He cares

Scripture says:

"Call to Me and I will answer you…"

That is a promise.

So when you pray, you are not speaking into emptiness.

You are speaking to a God who hears you.

Even when:

- your thoughts feel scattered
- your words feel simple
- your heart feels uncertain

You trust by faith that He is listening.

---

5. What Prayer Looks Like

Prayer can be very simple.

It may include:

- **Thanksgiving** — thanking God for who He is and what He has done
- **Confession** — honestly acknowledging sin
- **Requests** — bringing your needs before Him
- **Listening** — taking time to reflect and consider His Word

---

You do not need to include all of these every time.

Prayer is not structured for perfection.

It is shaped by relationship.

Sometimes prayer is:

- quiet
- brief
- simple

And that is enough.

Over time, you may find that prayer becomes:

- more natural
- more consistent
- more personal

Not because you have mastered it—

but because you are growing in relationship.

---

6. Why This Can Be Difficult

Even though prayer is simple, it can still feel challenging.

A. We Feel Uncertain

You may wonder:

- "Am I saying the right things?"
- "Does this matter?"

B. We Do Not See Immediate Results

You may pray and not see an immediate answer.
And you may quietly think:
"Is God really listening?"

But faith does not depend on what you can see.
It trusts what God has said.

C. We Feel Unworthy

At times, you may feel:

- "I shouldn't come to God right now"
- "I haven't been consistent"

But prayer is not based on your worthiness.
It is based on your relationship with Him.

---

7. A Biblical Example

We see a simple and honest example in the life of David.

Throughout the Psalms, David spoke openly to God.

He expressed:

- joy
- fear
- confusion
- gratitude

He did not try to present himself perfectly.
He came honestly.

We also see this in Jesus Christ.
Even Jesus spent time in prayer.
He withdrew to speak with the Father.

This shows us:
Prayer is not only for times of need—
it is part of a relationship.

---

8. What This Looks Like in Daily Life

Prayer does not need to be limited to a specific time or place.

It can become part of your daily life.

You might pray:

- at the start of your day
- when facing a decision
- in a moment of difficulty
- when you feel thankful

Sometimes it is as simple as:
"Lord, I need Your help right now."

Or:

"Thank You for what You've done."

Or:

"Help me to trust You in this."

These are real prayers.

And over time, these small moments begin to shape your awareness of God's presence.

---

9. Let This Settle Clearly

You do not need to:

- impress God
- find perfect words
- wait until you feel ready

You are invited to come as you are.

And just as you came to Him by faith—
you now speak with Him the same way.

---

10. Common Misunderstandings

X "I need to pray perfectly"

God listens to sincere hearts, not perfect words.

X "God only listens when I am doing well"

God invites you to come at all times.

X "If I don't see results, prayer isn't working"
God hears every prayer, even when answers take time.

X "Prayer must be long to matter"
Simple, honest prayer is meaningful.

---

11. God's Provision / Key Insight

God has not only spoken to you through His Word—

He has invited you to speak with Him.

You are not speaking to a distant God.

You are speaking to One who knows you and cares for you.

And as you trust Him:

- your confidence in prayer will grow
- your relationship with Him will deepen
- your heart will become more aligned with His

---

12. A Simple Step to Begin

Start simply.

Take a moment today and speak to God in your own words.

You might say:

"Lord, I want to learn to talk with You more. Help me to come to You honestly and trust that You hear me."

Then continue:

- one thought at a time
- one moment at a time

---

13. Linger Thought

You do not need special words to speak with God—

only a willing heart.

And as you come to Him by faith,

you will find that He is always ready to listen.

Concept 9 — Fellowship

Walking with Other Believers by Faith

---

1. The Core Truth

God has designed the Christian life to be lived in relationship with other believers. Fellowship is not optional—it is part of how we grow, are encouraged, and learn to walk with God together.

---

2. What Scripture Says

- "*And let's consider how to encourage one another in love and good deeds, not abandoning our own meeting together…*" — Hebrews 10:24–25
- "*For where two or three have gathered together in My name, I am there in their midst.*" — Matthew 18:20
- "*Be devoted to one another in brotherly love…*" — Romans 12:10
- "*Therefore encourage one another and build one another up…*" — 1 Thessalonians 5:11

---

3. Understanding the Truth

From the beginning, God did not intend for people to live in isolation.

This is true in life—and it is especially true in the Christian life.

When you come to Christ, you are not only brought into a relationship with God—

You are also brought into a relationship with others who belong to Him.

This is what the Bible calls **fellowship.**

Fellowship is more than:

- being around other believers
- attending a gathering
- having casual conversations

It is:

sharing life together in a way that centers on God

That means:

- encouraging one another
- supporting one another
- growing together

And over time, you begin to realize something important:

God often works in your life through other people

---

4. Why This Matters

The Christian life is not meant to be lived alone.

There are times when:

- you will be discouraged
- you will have questions
- you will struggle

And in those moments, it can be tempting to pull back.

To handle things quietly.

To keep things to yourself.

But Scripture says:

"Encourage one another… build one another up."

That is not something you can do alone.

Fellowship provides:

- encouragement when you are weak
- perspective when you are uncertain
- support when you are struggling

It is one of the ways God cares for you.

Not only directly—

but through others.

---

5. A Biblical Example

We see this clearly in the early believers described in Acts.

They were devoted to:

- teaching
- fellowship
- prayer

They shared life together.

They encouraged one another.

They grew together.

We also see this in the relationship between Paul and Timothy.

Paul encouraged Timothy.

He guided him.

He strengthened him.

This shows us something important:

Growth often happens in the context of relationships

---

6. Fellowship by Faith

Just as you walk with God by faith—

You also walk with others by faith

This is not always easy to recognize.

Because people are not perfect.

You may think:

- "What if they don't understand me?"
- "What if I feel uncomfortable?"
- "What if I'd rather just handle things on my own?"

But fellowship is not based on perfect people.

It is based on trusting that God works through imperfect people

---

This means:

- trusting that God can use others in your life
- choosing to be open and honest
- believing that encouragement matters

It is a step of faith to:

- share
- listen
- be known

But in that step, something begins to grow.

---

7. Why This Can Be Difficult

Even though fellowship is important, it is not always easy.

A. People Are Imperfect

Believers are still growing.

That means:

- misunderstandings happen
- disappointments occur

And when that happens, it can be tempting to withdraw.

B. It Requires Openness

Real fellowship involves:

- honesty
- humility
- willingness to be known

And that can feel uncomfortable.

You may think:

"It's easier to just keep things to myself"

C. We Feel We Should Handle Things Alone

You may think:

"I should be able to handle this myself."

But the Christian life was not designed that way.

---

8. What This Looks Like in Daily Life

Fellowship can take many forms.

It may include:

- spending time with other believers
- attending a church where God's Word is taught
- having conversations that encourage your faith
- praying with others

It does not need to be complicated.

It is simply:

sharing life with others who are also following Christ

Sometimes it is as simple as:

- listening
- encouraging
- being present

And over time, those simple moments begin to build something steady.

---

9. Let This Settle Clearly

You are not meant to walk this life alone.
God has placed others around you for a reason.

And just as you trust Him in your own walk—
you also trust Him to work through others

Even when it feels uncertain.
Even when it feels uncomfortable.

---

10. Common Misunderstandings

X "I can grow just as well on my own"
God uses others as part of your growth.

X "Fellowship is just being around people"
It is sharing life in a way centered on God.

X "If people fail me, fellowship isn't worth it"
People are imperfect—but God still works through them.

X "I need to have everything together first"
Fellowship is part of how you grow—not the result of it.

---

11. God's Provision / Key Insight

God has not only given you:

- His Word
- His Spirit

He has also given you:

other believers

They are not an extra part of the Christian life.

They are part of God's design for your growth

---

12. A Simple Step to Begin

Take one simple step:

- spend time with another believer
- ask a question
- share something honestly
- offer encouragement

You might pray:

"Lord, help me to walk with others and to trust how You are working through them."

---

13. Linger Thought

You are not meant to walk alone—
God has placed others beside you.
And as you walk together by faith,
you will grow stronger.

Concept 10 — Witnessing

Sharing Your Faith with Others by Faith

---

1. The Core Truth

God calls every believer to share the message of Christ with others. Witnessing is not about ability or pressure—it is about trusting God to work through you as you speak by faith.

---

2. What Scripture Says

- *"Go, therefore, and make disciples of all the nations…"* — Matthew 28:19–20
- *"But you will receive power when the Holy Spirit has come upon you; and you shall be My witnesses…"* — Acts 1:8
- *"Always be ready to make a defense to everyone who asks you to give an account for the hope that is in you…"* — 1 Peter 3:15
- *"How are they to believe in Him of whom they have not heard?"* — Romans 10:14

---

3. Understanding the Truth

When you came to Christ, something changed in your life.

You came to know:

- God's love
- the truth about sin

- the gift of salvation

And naturally, this raises a question:
"What about others?"

God's desire is not only that you know Him—
but that others come to know Him as well.

This is what we call **witnessing.**
It simply means:
sharing what you have come to know about Christ

It is not about having all the answers.
It is not about being an expert.

It is about:

- speaking honestly
- pointing others to Christ
- trusting God with the results

And often, it is much simpler than we imagine.

---

4. Witnessing by Faith

Just as you came to Christ by faith…
You share your faith the same way.

This is very important to understand.
Because this is where many believers hesitate.

You may find yourself thinking:

- "What if I don't say it right?"
- "What if I miss something important?"
- "What if I'm not ready?"

But witnessing is not based on:

- confidence in yourself
- perfect understanding
- having the right words every time

It is based on:

trusting that God can work through you

Scripture says:

"You will receive power… and you shall be My witnesses."

That means:

- God is with you
- God is working
- God uses what you say

Even when you feel:

- uncertain
- unprepared
- hesitant

There is often a quiet moment—
just before you speak—
where you must decide:

"Will I trust God here… or stay silent?"

Witnessing by faith is choosing to take that step.

---

5. A Biblical Example

We see this clearly in the life of Andrew.
After meeting Jesus, Andrew did something simple.
He went to his brother and said:
"We have found the Messiah."

He did not give a long explanation.
He simply shared what he had discovered.

We also see this in Samaritan woman.

After speaking with Jesus, she went back to her town and said:

"Come, see a man who told me everything I've done."

She did not have full understanding.
But she shared what she knew.

These examples show us:
Witnessing is often simple and personal

---

6. Why This Can Be Difficult

Even though witnessing is simple, it can feel challenging.

A. Fear of Saying the Wrong Thing

You may think:

- "What if I don't explain it well?"
- "What if I get something wrong?"

B. Fear of Rejection

You may wonder:

- "What will they think?"
- "What if they don't respond well?"

C. Feeling Unprepared

You may feel:

"I don't know enough yet."

And because of these things, it can feel easier to wait.

To say:

"Maybe later… when I'm more ready."

But witnessing is not about having everything figured out.

---

7. What This Looks Like in Daily Life

Witnessing often happens in simple ways.

It may look like:

- sharing what God has done in your life
- explaining the message of salvation
- answering a question
- inviting someone to learn more

Sometimes it begins with something as simple as:

"This is what I've come to understand…"

Or:

"This is how my life has changed…"

You are not trying to convince people on your own.

You are pointing them to Christ

And sometimes, you may not see any response right away.

But that does not mean nothing is happening.

---

8. Let This Settle Clearly

You are not responsible for the outcome.

You cannot:

- change hearts
- force understanding
- produce results

That is God's work.

Your part is simple:

- to be willing
- to speak
- and to trust Him

Even when:

- the conversation feels small
- the response feels unclear
- nothing seems to happen

You trust that God is working—
even when you cannot see it

---

9. Common Misunderstandings

X "I need to know everything first"
You can share what you already know.

X **"I must have the perfect words"**
God works through simple, sincere words.

X "It's my responsibility to make them believe"
Only God can change hearts.

X "If I feel nervous, I shouldn't speak"
You can act by faith even when you feel uncertain.

---

10. God's Provision / Key Insight

God has not asked you to do this alone.
He has given you:

- His Spirit — to guide and empower
- His Word — to give you truth
- His presence — to be with you

You are not sharing on your own.
God is working through you

---

11. A Simple Step to Begin

Take one simple step:
Think of one person in your life.

Pray:

"Lord, give me an opportunity to share, and help me to trust You when that moment comes."

Then be ready.
Not with pressure—
but with a willing heart

---

12. Linger Thought

You came to Christ by faith—
and now you share Him the same way.
Trusting that as you speak,
God is at work

Concept 11 — Obedience and Walking by Faith

Living in Response to God Day by Day

---

1. The Core Truth

Obedience is not how we earn God's acceptance—it is how we respond to Him. The Christian life is lived by faith, and obedience flows from trusting what God has said.

---

2. What Scripture Says

- *"If you love Me, you will keep My commandments."* — John 14:15
- *"But prove yourselves doers of the word, and not just hearers…"* — James 1:22
- *"And without faith it is impossible to please Him…"* — Hebrews 11:6
- *"So then, just as you received Christ Jesus as Lord, continue to walk in Him."* — Colossians 2:6

---

3. Understanding the Truth

At this point, you have seen:

- God's love
- The problem of sin
- Salvation through Christ
- Assurance and identity

- How to walk with God
- How to relate to others
- How to share your faith

And now, a final question naturally comes:

"How do I live this out consistently?"

The answer is:

Obedience—but understood in the right way

Obedience is often misunderstood.

Some think of it as:

- pressure
- performance
- trying to prove themselves

And because of that, it can begin to feel heavy.

You may even find yourself thinking:

- "Am I doing enough?"
- "Am I getting this right?"

But biblical obedience is not about earning something from God.

It is a response to what He has already done.

Jesus said:

"If you love Me, you will keep My commandments."

Notice the order:

- Love comes first
- Obedience follows

Obedience does not produce your relationship with God.

It flows out of it.

And that changes everything.

---

4. Obedience by Faith

This is where everything in the Christian life comes together.

Just as you came to Christ by faith…

You now walk in obedience the same way.

Scripture says:

"Just as you received Christ Jesus… continue to walk in Him."

How did you receive Him?

- not by effort
- not by performance
- but by faith

So how do you continue?

In the same way—by faith.

This is where many believers quietly struggle.

They begin by trusting Christ—

but then try to live the Christian life through effort alone.

They think:

- "Now it's up to me"
- "I need to carry this forward"

But the Christian life was never meant to be carried that way.

Obedience Is Trust in Action

When God says something in His Word, you respond by:

- believing it is true
- trusting that it is right
- choosing to act on it

Even when:

- it feels difficult
- it is not fully understood
- it goes against your natural instincts

That step—
that quiet decision to trust Him—
is obedience.

---

5. A Biblical Example

We see this clearly in the life of Abraham.

God called Abraham to go to a place he did not yet know.

Scripture tells us:

"By faith Abraham… obeyed."

He did not have:

- all the details
- a full explanation
- a clear picture of the outcome

But he trusted God.

And that trust led to obedience.

We also see this in Peter.

When Jesus told Peter to step out of the boat and walk on the water, Peter responded.

Not because it made sense.

But because he trusted the One who called him.

For a moment, he walked.

Not by ability—

but by trust.

These examples show us:

Obedience is not always about understanding everything—

it is about trusting God enough to take the next step.

---

6. Why This Can Be Difficult

Even though this is clear, it is not always easy.

A. We Fall Back into Self-Effort

You may begin to think:

- "I just need to do better"

- "I need to try harder"

And without realizing it, you shift from faith to effort.

B. We Want Complete Understanding First

You may feel:

"Once I fully understand, then I'll act."

But often, understanding grows after obedience.

C. We Fear Getting It Wrong

You may hesitate:

- "What if I fail?"
- "What if I don't do this well?"

But obedience is not about perfection.

It is about direction.

---

7. What This Looks Like in Daily Life

Obedience is not usually dramatic.

It is often simple and quiet.

It may look like:

- choosing to trust God's Word in a situation
- responding with patience instead of frustration
- speaking truth when it would be easier to stay silent
- taking a step you feel unsure about

In those moments, you may not feel strong.

You may not feel ready.

But you respond by faith:
"Lord, I trust You—and I will take this step."

That is obedience.

And over time, those small steps begin to shape your life.

---

8. Let This Settle Clearly

You are not obeying to:

- earn God's love
- secure your place with Him
- prove your worth

You are obeying because:
you already belong to Him.

And even when you fail—
you do not return to fear.
You return to Him.

The Christian life is not:

- perfect obedience

It is:
ongoing trust.

---

9. Common Misunderstandings

X "Obedience earns God's acceptance"

You are already accepted in Christ.

X "If I fail, I've lost everything"
Failure does not undo your relationship with God.

X "I must understand everything first"
Faith often comes before full understanding.

X "Obedience means perfection"
Obedience means trusting God and moving forward.

---

10. God's Provision / Key Insight

God has not asked you to obey on your own.
He has given you:

- His Spirit — to guide and strengthen you
- His Word — to show you what is true
- His grace — to restore you when you fail

You are not alone in this.
God is at work in you.

---

11. A Simple Step to Begin

Take one simple step today.
Ask:

- "What is one thing I know God is leading me to trust Him in?"

Then respond:
"Lord, I trust You. Help me take this step."

And take it—
not in your own strength,
but by faith.

---

12. Linger Thought

You began your walk with God by faith—
and you continue the same way.
Step by step, day by day,
trusting Him as you go.

Concept 12 — Walking by the Spirit

Living the Christian Life Through Dependence on God

---

1. The Core Truth

The Christian life is not lived by your own strength, but by the Spirit of God working in you—as you learn to depend on Him.

---

2. What Scripture Says

• "*But I say, walk by the Spirit, and you will not carry out the desire of the flesh.*" — Galatians 5:16

• "*I am the vine, you are the branches… apart from Me you can do nothing.*" — John 15:5

• "*For all who are being led by the Spirit of God, these are sons of God.*" — Romans 8:14

• "*For it is God who is at work in you, both to will and to work for His good pleasure.*" — Philippians 2:13

---

3. Understanding the Truth

When you trusted in Jesus Christ, you were not only forgiven—you were given new life.

Part of that new life is this:

God Himself now lives in you through His Spirit.

The Christian life, then, is not simply about trying to live better.

It is about learning to live in dependence on Him.

Jesus said, "apart from Me you can do nothing."

That is not meant to discourage you.

It is meant to direct you.

The life God calls you to live is not something you can produce on your own.

But it is something He is fully able to produce in you.

The question is not:

"Do I have the Spirit?"

If you are in Christ, you do.

The question becomes:

"Am I depending on Him?"

Walking by the Spirit is not a complicated process.

It is a relationship.

It is a moment-by-moment reliance on God—trusting Him to guide, to strengthen, and to work through you.

---

4. The Key Difference

There are two ways a believer may attempt to live the Christian life:

By self-effort

• Trying harder

• Relying on personal strength

• Measuring success by performance

By dependence on the Spirit

• Trusting God to work within you

• Relying on His strength

• Resting in His promises

The difference is not always visible on the outside

at first.

But over time, the results are very different.

Self-effort leads to frustration, weariness, and inconsistency.

Dependence on the Spirit leads to growth, steadiness, and quiet confidence in God.

---

5. What It Means to Walk by the Spirit

Walking by the Spirit is not about a special feeling or experience.

It is a simple, ongoing posture of the heart.

It means:

- Trusting God in each moment
- Looking to Him for strength
- Responding to His Word
- Yielding your choices to Him

Sometimes this will feel very clear.

Other times it may feel quiet and ordinary.

But it is real.

Just as you trusted Christ to save you, you now trust Him to lead you.

The same faith that began your relationship with God is the faith that continues it.

---

6. When We Fail

Even as believers, we will not walk perfectly.

There will be times when you rely on yourself instead of God.

Times when you make choices you know are not right.

When that happens, it is easy to feel:

• Discouraged
• Distant
• Unsure of what to do next

But God has not left you without direction.

Scripture says:

"If we confess our sins, He is faithful and righteous to forgive us our sins and to cleanse us from all unrighteousness." — 1 John 1:9

Confession is not a way to earn forgiveness.

It is a way of returning to honesty before God.

It is simply agreeing with Him about what is true.

And then—just as simply—you return to dependence.

Not trying harder.

Not starting over.

But trusting Him again.

---

7. What This Looks Like in Daily Life

Walking by the Spirit is not something reserved for certain moments.

It is meant to shape everyday life.

It may look like:

• Pausing to seek God's help before responding
• Trusting Him in a difficult situation
• Choosing what is right even when it is not easy
• Turning to Him when you feel weak

Most of the time, it will not feel dramatic.

It will feel steady.

Quiet.

Consistent.

Over time, you will begin to notice:

• Greater patience
• A growing desire for what is right
• A deeper awareness of God's presence

Not because you are trying harder—
But because He is at work within you.

---

8. Common Misunderstandings

X "This is only for certain Christians"

Every believer has the Spirit. This is for you.

X "I need a special experience to begin"

Walking by the Spirit begins with simple trust, not a special event.

X "If I were doing this right, it would feel different"

Feelings may come and go. Dependence is not based on emotion.

X "This means I will not struggle anymore"

Growth includes struggle. The difference is that you are no longer alone in it.

---

9. God's Provision / Key Insight

God has not only called you to live the Christian life—

He has provided everything needed to live it.

• His Spirit lives within you
• His Word guides you
• His grace sustains you

The Christian life is not something you accomplish

for God.

It is something God accomplishes in and through you as you trust Him.

---

10. A Simple Step to Begin

If you desire to walk by the Spirit, begin simply.

Turn to God in a quiet moment and acknowledge your need.

You might express the desire of your heart in a way like this—using your own words:

"Lord, I cannot live this life on my own. I am trusting You to guide me and strengthen me today. Help me to depend on You in each step."

The specific words are not what matter.

What matters is a heart that is turning to God in dependence and trust.

Then move forward—

Not in your own strength,

But in quiet reliance on Him.

---

11. Linger Thought

The Christian life is not lived by trying harder—

It is lived by trusting deeper.

Conclusion - Continuing the Walk

You have now walked through a series of foundational truths.

You have seen:

- God's love and His desire for you
- The reality of sin and our need
- The provision of salvation through Christ
- The assurance that you belong to Him
- Your identity in Christ
- How to walk with God day by day
- How He speaks through His Word
- How you speak with Him in prayer
- The importance of fellowship
- The call to share your faith
- And what it means to live in obedience
- Walking by the Spirit

That is a lot to take in.

And it is important to remember:

You are not expected to master all of this at once.

A **Life, Not a Lesson**

The Christian life is not something you complete.

It is something you continue.

It is not:

- a lesson to finish
- a system to perfect
- a standard to reach

It is:

a relationship you grow in

And like any relationship, it develops over time.

It deepens gradually.

It becomes more steady as you continue.

There Will Be Different Days

There will be days when things feel clear.

There will also be days when:

- you feel uncertain
- you struggle
- you do not feel strong

There may even be days when you wonder:

"Am I really growing at all?"

None of this means something is wrong.

It means you are learning.

Returning Again and Again

You will find that the Christian life often comes back to simple things.

Again and again, you will return to:

- trusting what God has said

- speaking with Him in prayer
- taking one step of obedience
- leaning on Him in weakness

These are not small things.
They are the very foundation of your walk.

And each time you return—
you are walking by faith

When You Feel Discouraged

There may be times when you feel:

- "I should be further along"
- "I've struggled with this again"
- "I don't feel like I'm growing"

In those moments, it is easy to become discouraged.

Or to begin to measure yourself by how you feel.

But instead, remember what is true:

- Your relationship with God is secure
- Your identity in Christ has not changed
- God is still at work in you

Even when you do not feel it.
Even when you do not see it clearly.

You do not need to start over.
You simply return to Him.

You Are Not Alone

God has not left you to walk this path on your own.

He has given you:

- His Spirit — to guide and strengthen you
- His Word — to give you truth
- Other believers — to walk beside you

And often, He will remind you of His presence—through these very things.

You are supported.

You are cared for.

You are not alone.

A Simple Way Forward

If everything feels like a lot, bring it back to something simple.

Each day, take one step.

- trust God for today
- spend a little time in His Word
- speak with Him honestly
- take one step of obedience

You do not need to do everything at once.

You do not need to move quickly.

Just take the next step.

Not perfectly.
But faithfully.

The Heart of It All

If you remember nothing else, remember this:
You began your relationship with God by faith.
And you continue the same way.

Not by striving.
Not by pressure.
Not by trying to become strong on your own.

But by trusting Him.

And that trust will grow—
step by step,
day by day.

Keep Walking

This is not the end.
It is the beginning of a clearer path.
A steadier path.
A path of learning to walk with God.

And as you continue—
step by step, day by day—
you will find that He is faithful

Final Thought

You do not need to have everything figured out.
You only need to keep walking—
by faith.

Appendix A — Key Bible Verses to Remember

Truth to Return to in Every Season

There are times in the Christian life when you may feel:

- uncertain
- discouraged
- weak
- in need of direction

In those moments, it is helpful to return to what God has said.

These verses are not meant to be memorized all at once.

They are here so that, over time, you can:

return to them, reflect on them, and learn to trust them—by faith.

Assurance — Knowing You Belong to God

- "These things I have written to you who believe in the name of the Son of God, so that you may know that you have eternal life." — 1 John 5:13
- "My sheep listen to My voice… and I give them eternal life, and they will never perish; and no one will snatch them out of My hand." — John 10:27–28
- "Therefore there is now no condemnation at all for those who are in Christ Jesus." — Romans 8:1

Identity in Christ — Who You Are Now

- "Therefore if anyone is in Christ, this person is a new creation…" — 2 Corinthians 5:17
- "But as many as received Him, to them He gave the right to become children of God…" — John 1:12
- "For you are all sons and daughters of God through faith in Christ Jesus." — Galatians 3:26

Walking by Faith — Daily Trust

- "For we walk by faith, not by sight." — 2 Corinthians 5:7
- "Trust in the Lord with all your heart and do not lean on your own understanding."
  — Proverbs 3:5–6
- "And without faith it is impossible to please Him…" — Hebrews 11:6

God's Word — Truth That Guides You

- "Your word is a lamp to my feet and a light to my path." — Psalm 119:105
- "Sanctify them in the truth; Your word is truth." — John 17:17
- "All Scripture is inspired by God…"
  — 2 Timothy 3:16

Prayer — Speaking with God

- "Call to Me and I will answer you…" — Jeremiah 33:3
- "Be anxious for nothing, but in everything by prayer… let your requests be made known to God." — Philippians 4:6–7
- "If we ask anything according to His will, He hears us." — 1 John 5:14

Strength in Weakness — When You Feel Discouraged

- "My grace is sufficient for you, for power is perfected in weakness." — 2 Corinthians 12:9
- "Come to Me, all who are weary and burdened, and I will give you rest." — Matthew 11:28
- "The Lord is near to the brokenhearted…" — Psalm 34:18

Obedience — Trusting God's Way

- "If you love Me, you will keep My commandments." — John 14:15
- "But prove yourselves doers of the word…" — James 1:22
- "Just as you received Christ Jesus as Lord, continue to walk in Him." — Colossians 2:6

God's Presence — You Are Not Alone

- "I will never desert you, nor will I ever abandon you." — Hebrews 13:5
- "And behold, I am with you always…" — Matthew 28:20
- "The Lord is my shepherd, I will not be in need." — Psalm 23:1

Sharing Your Faith — God Working Through You

- "You will receive power… and you shall be My witnesses…" — Acts 1:8
- "How are they to believe in Him of whom they have not heard?" — Romans 10:14
- "Always be ready to give an answer…" — 1 Peter 3:15

A Final Word

You do not need to remember every verse.

You do not need to use them all at once.

But as you grow, you will find that certain verses begin to stay with you.

They come to mind:

- in moments of uncertainty
- in times of need
- when you are seeking direction

And in those moments, you are not relying on your own thoughts—

you are returning to what God has said.

Linger Thought

When your thoughts feel uncertain,
return to what is certain—
the Word of God.

Appendix B — When You Struggle

Returning to God When Things Feel Difficult

There will be times in your Christian life when things feel difficult.

You may experience:

- discouragement
- distance
- confusion
- failure

You may even begin to wonder:

- "Am I doing something wrong?"
- "Why does this feel so hard?"
- "Shouldn't I be further along?"

It is important to understand:

These moments are not unusual.

They are part of learning to walk with God.

When You Feel Distant from God

There may be times when you feel:

- disconnected
- quiet inside
- unsure of God's presence

You may think:

"God feels far away."

But your relationship with God is not based on what you feel.

It is based on what He has promised.

Scripture says:

"I will never desert you, nor will I ever abandon you." — Hebrews 13:5

Even when you do not feel it:

He is still with you.

In those moments, do something simple:

- return to His Word
- speak with Him honestly
- take a small step forward

Not because you feel strong—

but because you trust Him.

When You Fall into Sin

There may be times when you fail.

You may say something you regret.

You may act in a way you know is not right.

And afterward, you may feel:

- guilt
- disappointment
- distance

You may even think:

"I've taken a step backward."

But this is a very important moment.

Because your response matters.

Instead of pulling away from God—

return to Him.

Scripture says:

"If we confess our sins, He is faithful and righteous, so that He will forgive us…" — 1 John 1:9

You do not need to hide.

You do not need to wait.

You do not need to fix yourself first.

You come honestly.

You confess.

And you trust His forgiveness—by faith.

When You Feel Discouraged

There may be times when you feel:

- "I'm not growing"
- "This is harder than I expected"
- "I keep struggling with the same things"

Discouragement can come quietly.

And over time, it can begin to weigh on you.

In those moments, remember:

- growth takes time
- change is often gradual
- God is patient

Scripture says:

"My grace is sufficient for you…" — 2 Corinthians 12:9

You may not see everything changing at once.

But God is still at work in you.

When You Feel Unsure What to Do

There will be times when you simply do not know what to do next.

You may feel:

- uncertain
- unsure of direction
- hesitant to move forward

In those moments, come back to what is clear.

You do not need to see everything.

You only need to take the next step.

Scripture says:

"Your word is a lamp to my feet and a light to my path." — Psalm 119:105

God often guides one step at a time.

A Simple Pattern to Follow

When you struggle, return to something simple:

1. Be honest with God
2. Tell Him what you are feeling
3. Return to what is true
4. Read a portion of Scripture
5. Take one step forward
6. Even if it feels small

You do not need to fix everything at once.
You simply return—and continue.

Let This Settle Clearly

Struggle does not mean failure.
Difficulty does not mean something is wrong.

Often, it means:
You are learning to depend on God more deeply.

And each time you return to Him—
you are walking by faith.

A Final Word

You will not walk this path perfectly.
But you do not need to.

God is not asking for perfection.
He is inviting you to keep coming back.

Again and again.

Linger Thought

When you struggle, do not pull away—
return to Him.
And as you do,
you will find that His grace is still there.

Appendix C — A Simple Guide to Prayer

Learning to Speak with God Day by Day

Prayer is one of the simplest parts of the Christian life—

and at the same time, one of the most meaningful.

You do not need special words.
You do not need a perfect structure.
You do not need to feel ready.

You simply come to God—and speak.

What Prayer Is

Prayer is not a performance.
It is not something you do to impress God.
It is:
a conversation with Him

You speak.
He hears.

Even when your words are simple.
Even when your thoughts feel scattered.

You are speaking to a God who knows you—and cares for you.

Coming to God by Faith

You do not see God.

You do not hear Him audibly.

Yet you come to Him anyway.

Why?

Because you trust that He is there—and that He hears you.

Scripture says:

"Call to Me and I will answer you…" —Jeremiah 33:3

So when you pray, you are not speaking into emptiness.

You are speaking to God—by faith.

A Simple Way to Begin

If you are unsure how to pray, start with something simple.

You can use this pattern if it helps:

---

1. Thank God

Take a moment to thank Him.

You might say:

"Lord, thank You for who You are… and for what You have done."

---

2. Speak Honestly

Tell Him what is on your heart.

- your concerns
- your questions
- your struggles

You might say:

"Lord, I'm not sure what to do about this…"

---

3. Ask for Help

Bring your needs to Him.

You might say:

"Lord, I need Your help. Please guide me."

---

4. Trust Him

Even if nothing feels different right away, you choose to trust Him.

You might say:

"Lord, I trust You—even if I don't see the answer yet."

When Prayer Feels Difficult

There will be times when prayer does not feel easy.

You May Not Know What to Say

That is okay.

You can begin with something simple:

"Lord, I don't know what to say—but I want to come to You."

You May Feel Distracted

Your thoughts may wander.
That is normal.

When it happens, gently return your attention.
You do not need to start over.

You May Not Feel Anything

Sometimes prayer feels quiet.
You may think:
"Is anything happening?"

But prayer is not based on what you feel.
It is based on what God has said.

He hears you.

Short Prayers for Everyday Moments

Prayer does not need to be long.
Often, the most meaningful prayers are simple.

You might pray:

- "Lord, help me right now."
- "Thank You for this moment."
- "Give me wisdom here."
- "Help me trust You."

These are real prayers.

Growing in Prayer

Over time, prayer becomes more natural.

Not because you have mastered it—

but because you are growing in your relationship with God.

You may find that:

- you speak more freely
- you return to Him more often
- you become more aware of His presence

This growth is gradual.

And that is okay.

A Simple Daily Practice

If you are unsure where to begin, try something simple:

- Take a few minutes each day
- Speak honestly with God
- Read a small portion of Scripture
- Respond in prayer

It does not need to be long.

It does not need to be perfect.

Just be consistent.

Let This Settle Clearly

You do not need to:

- impress God
- say everything perfectly
- wait until you feel ready

You are invited to come as you are.

And just as you came to Him by faith—
you now speak with Him the same way.

Linger Thought

You do not need perfect words to speak with God—
only a willing heart.
And as you come to Him by faith,
you will find that He is always ready to listen.

Appendix D — How to Begin Reading the Bible

Learning to Hear from God Day by Day

Reading the Bible can feel overwhelming at first.

You may wonder:

- "Where do I start?"
- "How much should I read?"
- "What if I don't understand it?"

These are normal questions.

And it is important to remember:

You do not need to understand everything at once to begin.

Why the Bible Matters

The Bible is not just a book of information.

It is:

God's Word given to you

Through it, God shows you:

- who He is
- what is true
- how to walk with Him

Scripture says:

"Your word is a lamp to my feet and a light to my path." — Psalm 119:105

It gives you light—
not for everything at once,
but for the next step.

Where to Begin

If you are just starting, it helps to begin in places that are clear and foundational.

A Simple Starting Point

- The Gospel of John
- → to understand who Jesus is
- The Psalms
- → to see how people speak honestly with God
- Philippians or Ephesians
- → to understand the Christian life

You do not need to read large sections.
A few verses at a time is enough.

How to Read Simply

Reading the Bible does not need to be complicated.
Here is a simple way to begin:

---

1. Read a Short Passage

Take a few verses.
Read slowly.

---

2. Ask One or Two Questions

- What does this show me about God?
- What is something I can trust here?

You do not need to find everything.
Just look for one clear truth.

---

3. Think About It

Pause for a moment.
Let it settle.

---

4. Respond

You might:

- pray about what you read
- take one small step to apply it
- simply trust what it says

Reading by Faith

Just as you came to Christ by faith…
You now read His Word the same way.

There will be times when:

- you do not fully understand
- nothing feels especially meaningful
- you are unsure what to take from it

In those moments, it is easy to think:
"This may not be helping."

But the Word of God does not depend on your feelings.

So you continue:

- reading

- listening
- trusting

By faith.

And over time, something begins to happen.

- your thinking becomes clearer
- your understanding grows
- your responses begin to change

Often slowly.

But steadily.

When It Feels Difficult

There will be times when reading feels hard.

You May Not Understand Everything

That is normal.

Understanding grows over time.

You May Feel Inconsistent

You may start and stop.

That is okay.

Just begin again.

You May Feel Like It Isn't Doing Much

But God's Word is still working—

even when you do not see it immediately.

A Simple Daily Plan

If you would like a starting point:

- Read a small portion each day
- Keep it simple and consistent
- Do not rush

Even 5–10 minutes is meaningful.

Let This Settle Clearly

You are not trying to master the Bible.

You are learning to listen to God.

And just as you came to Him by faith—

you now trust what He has said the same way.

A Final Encouragement

Do not be discouraged if it feels slow.

Do not be discouraged if you do not understand everything.

What matters is this:

You are coming to God—and that matters.

Linger Thought

You do not need to understand everything to begin—

only to take the next step.

And as you return to God's Word,

it will begin to shape your life.

Where to Go From Here

Taking the Next Step in Your Walk with God

You have now read through these foundational truths.

You have seen what God has done, what He has said, and how to begin walking with Him.

The next step is not to try to do everything at once.

It is to begin—simply and steadily.

---

1. Keep Walking by Faith

The Christian life begins by faith.

And it continues the same way.

You do not need to feel strong.

You do not need to have everything figured out.

You simply trust Him—

one step at a time.

---

2. Spend Time in God's Word

Make time, even in small amounts, to read the Bible.

You do not need to read a lot.

Start with a few verses.

Read slowly.

Think about what God is saying.

Over time, His Word will:

- guide your thinking
- shape your decisions
- strengthen your faith

---

3. Speak with God in Prayer

Prayer does not need to be complicated.
Speak with God honestly.

- thank Him
- bring your concerns
- ask for help

You are not speaking into emptiness.
He hears you.

---

4. Connect with Other Believers

The Christian life is not meant to be lived alone.

Look for:

- a Bible-believing church
- other believers to spend time with
- opportunities to learn and grow together

It may take time to find the right place.
Do not be discouraged—keep looking.

---

5. Take Simple Steps of Obedience

As you learn from God's Word, take small steps to follow Him.

You do not need to do everything at once.

You do not need to be perfect.

Just take the next step.

---

6. Keep Growing

Growth takes time.

There will be:

- clear days
- difficult days
- steady progress
- moments of struggle

All of this is part of the journey.

What matters is not how fast you grow—
but that you continue.

---

7. When You Struggle, Return

There will be times when you feel:

- discouraged
- uncertain
- distant

When that happens:

- return to God
- return to His Word
- take one step forward

You do not need to start over.
You simply continue.

A Final Encouragement

You do not need to carry everything at once.
You do not need to do this perfectly.

You are learning.
You are growing.
You are walking with God.

And as you continue—
step by step, day by day—
you will find that He is faithful.

Linger Thought

You do not need to know everything about the path ahead—
only to take the next step.
And as you do,
God will lead you.

Continue Your Journey in the Bible

If this book has helped you begin reading and understanding the Bible, there is a natural next step: Learning how to walk with God day by day.
You do not need to take everything in at once.
Simply continue—one step at a time.

Start Here — Learning to Read and Understand
<u>How to Read and Understand the Bible</u>
A simple, step-by-step guide designed to help you begin reading Scripture with clarity and confidence.

Next Step — Learning to Walk with God
<u>Walking With God</u>
Biblical Foundations for New Believers
Once you begin to understand the Bible, the next question often becomes: *How do I live this out?*
Walking With God provides a clear and steady introduction to the Christian life—helping you understand what it means to grow, trust God, and take simple steps forward each day.

Build a Strong Foundation

<u>The Bible Unlocked</u>

A clear guide to all 66 books of the Bible, helping you understand what each book says, why it matters, and how it fits together.

Grow in Understanding

<u>What the Bible Is Really All About</u>

A devotional overview of the entire Bible, showing how each book fits into God's plan.

<u>Handling God's Word with Care</u>

A thoughtful guide to studying the Bible faithfully and carefully.

Know God More Deeply

The Attributes of God

A clear and personal look at who God is and how His character shapes our lives.

Walk Through Scripture

<u>Walking Through the Psalms</u>
A slow and thoughtful journey through selected Psalms, focused on truth, trust, and praise.
<u>That You May Believe</u>
A reflective walk through the Gospel of John, focusing on the life and purpose of Jesus.

Learn from Biblical Lives
<u>Lives of Faith</u>
Reflections on key people in the Bible and how God worked through their lives.

For Families and Foundations
<u>Foundations of Faith</u>
A clear and steady guide to core biblical truths for individuals and families.

Reflect and Remember

Remembering God's Help — Stone by Stone

A collection of Scripture-based reflections focused on God's faithfulness in daily life.

Continue reading.
Continue growing.
Continue walking with God.

How to Trust Jesus as Your Savior

The most important decision any person will ever make is what they do with Jesus Christ.

Becoming a Christian is not about joining a religion, trying harder, or becoming good enough. It is about trust — trusting Jesus.

The Bible tells us that every one of us has fallen short of God's perfect standard. We have all sinned. That sin separates us from God, and left on its own, it leads to death — not only physical death, but eternal separation from the God who made us and loves us.

But God did not leave us there.

In His great love, God sent His Son, Jesus Christ, to do for us what we could never do for ourselves. Jesus lived a perfect life, willingly died on the cross for our sins, was buried, and rose again. His resurrection is God's assurance that sin and death have been defeated.

The Bible speaks of this love in simple and beautiful words:

"For God so loved the world, that He gave His only begotten Son, that whoever believes in Him shall not perish, but have eternal life."

— John 3:16

Becoming a Christian is not a long process — it is a moment of trust. It is the moment when you personally rely on Jesus Christ alone to save you. It is choosing, from the heart, to say something like this:

"Jesus, I know that I cannot save myself. I believe You died for me and rose again. I place my trust in You right now to forgive my sins and give me eternal life."

The words themselves are not what save you. What matters is the posture of your heart — trusting Jesus alone to save you.

That is faith. You do not need to walk an aisle, join a church, or perform good works to be saved. Salvation is God's free gift, received by faith alone.

If you have never trusted Jesus Christ, you can do so right now — wherever you are, in the quiet of your heart. The moment you place your trust in Him, God declares you forgiven, gives you eternal life, and welcomes you as His child.

And if you have already trusted Christ, keep growing. Walk with Him day by day. Read His Word. Learn to rely on His Spirit. Remember — the Christian life begins with grace, and it continues by grace.

Scripture References

🕮 **Romans 3:23**

"for all have sinned and fall short of the glory of God,,"

🕮 **Romans 6:23**

"For the wages of sin is death, but the free gift of God is eternal life in Christ Jesus our Lord"

🕮 **1 Peter 3:18**

"For Christ also suffered once for sins, the righteous for the unrighteous, that he might bring us to God, being put to death in the flesh but made alive in the spirit,"

🕮 **John 3:16**

"For God so loved the world, that he gave his only Son, that whoever believes in him should not perish but have eternal life."

🕮 **Romans 10:9–10, 13**

9 because, if you confess with your mouth that Jesus is Lord and believe in your heart that God raised him from the dead, you will be saved. 10 For with the heart one believes and is justified, and with the mouth one confesses and is saved.

13 For "everyone who calls on the name of the Lord will be saved."

These verses explain the simple and wonderful truth of salvation by grace through faith in Jesus

About the Author

Russell McFall has spent a lifetime helping others understand truth in a clear and practical way. With a background in software development and many years serving in children's ministry, he has always had a desire to take complex ideas and make them simple and accessible.

Russell and his wife homeschooled their children for 16 years, where many of his earliest stories and teachings began as conversations around the table or lessons shared at home. Over time, those simple beginnings grew into a deeper calling to write—focusing on faith, character, and the importance of understanding God's Word.

His goal in writing is not to overwhelm, but to guide—to help readers see what Scripture says and to walk with God in a steady, thoughtful way.

Russell continues to write with a heart for encouraging others, especially those who are new in their faith, to grow in clarity, confidence, and a daily walk with God.

Also by Russell McFall

Ordained Path Books

Clean Science Fiction and Inspirational Writing for Thoughtful Readers

---

Contemporary Fiction and Short Stories

Stories of Community, Memory, and Hope

- **Squirrel Creek Estates — Where the Porch Lights Stay On**

The Space Cadet Richard Series

Where the Legacy Began

- **The Final Countdown**
- **The Dunes of Dinkytown**
- **The Mastermind's Maze**

The Space Cadet Legacy Series

Over 30 novels of courage, friendship, and discovery — including

- **The First Gate**
- **Welcome Back, Player**
- **Flibber's Journey Home**
- **Stronger Together**
- **Phasegate Rising**

(New missions continuing.)

Literary Humor and Reflections

Serious Nonsense — Sanity Sold Separately

Devotional and Reflection Books

- **Remembering God's Help — Stone by Stone**
- **Attributes of God**
- **This Is My Story, This Is My Song**
- **Lives of Faith**
- **Foundations of Faith**
- **The Bible Unlocked: Who, What, Why, Where, When & How of Every Bible Book**
- **How to Read and Understand the Bible**
- **Walking Through the Psalms**

Russell McFall writes clean fiction and thoughtful reflections designed to uplift the heart, sharpen the mind, and remind every reader that light still wins.

www.ingramcontent.com/pod-product-compliance
Lightning Source LLC
LaVergne TN
LVHW010703110826
845149LV00014B/3206

* 9 7 8 1 9 7 2 7 2 4 1 6 3 *